WE ARE CALLED

TO BE A

MOVEMENT

REVEREND DR.
WILLIAM J. BARBER II

D0950620

Library of Congress Cataloging-in-Publication Data is available.

ISBN 978-1-5235-1124-2

Design by Sarah Smith
Cover photo credit: Tanor/Shutterstock

All quoted scripture is from The Message or the New International
Version of the Holy Bible or is Rev. Dr. Barber's own interpretation.

Workman books are available at special discounts when purchased in
bulk for premiums and sales promotions as well as for fund-raising or
educational use. Special editions or book excerpts can also be created
to specification. For details, contact the Special Sales Director at the
address below, or send an email to specialmarkets@workman.com.

Workman Publishing Co., Inc.
225 Varick Street
New York, NY 10014-4381
workman.com

WORKMAN is a registered trademark of Workman Publishing Co., Inc.

Printed in the United States of America
First printing April 2020

10 9 8 7 6 5 4 3 2 1

A version of this sermon was first delivered on Sunday morning, June 3, 2018, at the National Cathedral in Washington, DC.

I am a preacher and the son of a preacher. I know many people in America today have good reasons not to trust a preacher. But I still believe in the prophetic power of the Bible, a book my father said you can't read honestly without also making a commitment to work for justice. So I'd like to begin with two pieces of ancient wisdom from the sacred texts of my tradition. The first is from Psalm 118:

> *The stone that the builders rejected*
> *has become the cornerstone!*
> *This is God's work.*
> *And it is marvelous in our eyes!*
> *This is the day that the LORD has made—*
> *let us rejoice and be glad in it!*

The second text comes from Jesus's very first sermon as recounted in the Gospel of Luke, chapter 4:

> *Jesus came to Nazareth where he had*
> *been raised. As he always did on the*

Sabbath, he went to the meeting place.
When he stood up to read, he was handed
the scroll of the prophet Isaiah. Unrolling
the scroll, he found the place where it was
written,

God's Spirit is on me;
   he's chosen me to preach the Message of
   good news to the poor,
Sent me to announce pardon to prisoners
   and recovery of sight to the blind,
To set the burdened and battered free, to
   announce, "This is God's time to shine!"

He rolled up the scroll, handed it back to
the assistant, and sat down. Every eye

*in the place was on him, intent. Then he
started in, "You've just heard Scripture
make history. It came true just now in
this place."*

I want to hold these two texts together—
to read Jesus's inaugural sermon in light
of the Psalmist's insight about those
who have been rejected. Psalms were the
freedom songs of the movement Jesus
was born into, and just as the songs of
the freedom movement prepare our
spirits to hear a prophetic word of truth
in today's movements for justice, the
Psalmist's song tunes our ear to hear the

transformative truth of Jesus's message. And the message is this:

The rejected must lead the revival for love and justice.

The cornerstone is that part of the foundation upon which the whole building stands. And the Psalmist says, speaking metaphorically of how we view human beings in society, that it is God's intent that the stones that were once seen as unfit to be a part of the architecture—the stones that were once thrown away or kept in the quarry—

have now been called to be the most important stones. The rejected stones make the best cornerstones. The rejected stones actually make the best foundation holders. And whenever you see rejected stones becoming the focus of society, it is the Lord's doing.

This psalm is a song Jesus would have known well as a brown-skinned Palestinian Jew who grew up practicing Passover, because Psalm 118 was the last of the Hallel Psalms sung on holy days. Perhaps Jesus had it in his spirit when he got up to preach the prophet Isaiah in the

THE REJECTED MUST LEAD THE REVIVAL FOR LOVE AND JUSTICE.

ghetto of Nazareth. Jesus's first sermon was not in Jerusalem—not in the well of Congress—but in the rejected and despised place called Nazareth.

"Can anything good come out of Nazareth?" the people asked.

In Nazareth Jesus announced, "The spirit of the Lord is upon me to proclaim good news to the poor." The Kingdom of God is at hand. A whole new world is possible. Jesus says, "I have come to reconstruct everything."

But note where he starts this reconstruction—with the poor. The Greek word is *ptokos*. It means those who have been made poor by economic systems of exploitation. Jesus's reconstruction project begins with good news to the poor and the brokenhearted and the bruised and the battered and all of those made to feel like they are not accepted. Jesus is explicit in his commitment to begin with the rejected.

In Caesar's world, where narcissistic leaders only cared about the grand and the greedy, the pompous and the pretentious, Jesus announces a revival led by and among the rejected. Caesar, who loved to put his face on money and buildings; Caesar, who catered to the greedy and led by fear and political shenanigans. Into Caesar's world—at that particular historical moment—Jesus announced prophetically that we are called to be a movement led by and with the poor.

And he was almost killed that day by religious leaders who had themselves rejected the poor.

These two Scriptures, while ancient, speak powerfully to our present. The context in which the Psalmist wrote and Jesus preached was one of a politics rooted in greed and not grace; a politics rooted in lust and not love. Both Jesus and the Psalmist spoke of the rejected because rejection had been embraced by the narcissistic powers of their day. In the Psalmist's day, it was the kings and false prophets of Israel. In Jesus's day, it was Caesar and the paid religionists who promoted an agenda that led to rejection, poverty, brokenness, and communities of the unaccepted. We miss the point of these texts if we don't see that the rejected they speak of were then—as they are now—victims of calculated and callous public policy. The rejected, the poor, the broken, the unaccepted were not in their condition because of their individual moral failings, but because of a society that had decided some people could be overlooked and left behind.

In a society with a narcissistic egotist clinging to power and political office, how strange it would have been for someone like Jesus to declare that the rejected would lead the revival—that the chief cornerstones would come from among the rejected. How strange in that context for someone to declare, "Blessed are the poor!"

Cicero called the poor in the Roman Empire "the dregs of society." The poor and the broken and the unaccepted were seen as burdens, not the honored ones. But Jesus puts these same poor people at the center of God's agenda for the world. In his very first sermon and in his last, at both the beginning and the end of his ministry, Jesus is empowering the poor

GOD USES THE REJECTED TO LEAD THE MORAL REVIVAL.

to stand up and to challenge systems that have caused rejection, bruising, and poverty.

By the Spirit of God—not by a poll, not by a certain consensus, not based on what the CNN of that day said—by the Spirit of God, Jesus announces a new politics has come into the earth. Both the Psalmist and the Savior question the politics of rejection. Together they call for a moral revival and a revolution of values.

The point at the heart of both Psalm 118 and Luke 4 echoes throughout

Scripture. We can't understand how God could use so many outsiders and misfits throughout the Scriptures, apart from the insight that God uses the rejected to lead the moral revival of nations.

It's why God speaks to Moses—the one with a stutter—and calls him to be spokesman for a people hard-pressed under Pharaoh. Because rejected stones make the best cornerstones.

It's why little David—the youngest and the shortest of all Jesse's sons—is the one to bring down the mighty Goliath.

Because rejected stones make the best cornerstones.

It's why Sisera, that great warrior, fell at the hand of Jael—a housekeeper who didn't even have a union to join. Because rejected stones make the best cornerstones.

And it's why, when Jesus was born in Bethlehem, the angels didn't show up to tell the mayor or the governor or the dean of the local university. No, "glad tidings of great joy" were proclaimed to the undocumented migrant farm workers, keeping watch over their flocks by night. Because rejected stones make the best cornerstones in the long song that Scripture sings.

More than two thousand times in Scripture, the Spirit of God speaks about how the rejected and their allies in the faith must prophetically challenge religious and political institutions. It is one of the most consistent themes throughout the Bible.

"Woe to those who make unjust laws, and to those who issue oppressive decrees, to deprive the poor of their rights and

REJECTED STONES MAKE THE BEST CONERSTONES.

withhold justice from the oppressed of my people," the prophet Isaiah says (Is 10:1). Ezekiel points to politicians who pass unjust laws and says they are "like wolves tearing their prey; they shed blood and kill people to make unjust gain" (Ez 22:27). And while God is looking for someone who will tell the truth about what is going on, Ezekiel points out how the court prophets "whitewash these deeds for them by false visions and lying divinations. They say, 'This is what the Sovereign Lord says,' when the LORD has not spoken" (Ez 22:28).

The prophet Jeremiah hears the Word of the Lord call him to go in person to the royal palace—not to send a messenger or a tweet. No, the prophet is sent to declare in person: "Do what is just and right. Rescue from the hand of the oppressor the one who has been robbed. Do no wrong or violence to the foreigner, the fatherless, or the widow, and do not shed innocent blood in this place" (Jer 22:3).

Jesus says in Matthew 25:45 that nations will be judged by whether we care for Jesus himself when he comes to us poor and homeless, sick and sore, as a prisoner or a refugee. "When you did not do it unto the least of these, you did not do it unto me," Jesus says.

The Bible does not invite us into some otherworldly journey or a mere praise party for a private society of me, myself, and I. No, we are called to be a movement for wholeness in a broken world and to stand for justice, so help us God.

In America's long story, we have a lot of stones that have been rejected. Policy violence and rejection have too often

WE ARE CALLED TO BE A MOVEMENT FOR WHOLENESS IN A BROKEN WORLD.

been our legacy. And often, in spite of the calling of the Spirit and instruction of the Scripture, that legacy has been endorsed by the church. Think, if you will, of the Trail of Tears, the rejection of America's Native indigenous people and the genocide of those folk. In America's story, they have been rejected stones. Think of the rejection of Black people's humanity—not just slavery, but *chattel* slavery, reducing human beings to nothing more than mere property and animals. Think how even in the original writing of the Constitution, women were rejected and poor white men who didn't have land were also rejected. We must be honest about these foundations and not think that there is some great day behind us when all was well.

We must be honest about the foundations of the political and economic systems we call America. I love America because of her potential. But I know that America will never complete the work of reconstruction—will never even get close to being a more perfect union—until we are honest about her past and the politics of rejection. And as a preacher, Lord help me, I must tell the truth about how the Christian faith has been used to whitewash the rejection that stains our nation's soul.

My brother who happens to be white, Jonathan Wilson-Hartgrove, is a Baptist preacher from the South. When I met him 20 years ago, he was working for Strom Thurmond and trying to climb the ranks of the religious right. But he saw the lie of divide-and-conquer politics— how the rejected get pitted against one another again and again. Now Jonathan is part of the movement to reconstruct American democracy, talking to white

Christians about how to get free from the habits of what he calls "slaveholder religion" in his book, *Reconstructing the Gospel: Finding Freedom from Slaveholder Religion.*

Jonathan writes about how slave masters paid preachers to twist the Scriptures against abolition, turning the message of Jesus against itself. He says in his book:

> *The sin that ripped the gospel in two—the spiritual root of our political divisions and class disparities—is a lie that was told centuries ago to justify*

owning, using, and abusing other human beings . . . we live in a society that continues to be divided, and we are, each and every one of us, divided ourselves at times.

We must tell the truth. The hardness of heart that we still see rejecting some people is not just the words of racism, but the works of racism. In fact, if you're not careful, you'll get caught up in the words of racism and miss the works of racism because some people who engage in the works of racism never use the words. But if we are honest about this past, we can see these same patterns repeating themselves in the present.

As a Christian preacher I want to speak where the Bible speaks and to declare in this moment that the politics of rejection is not a past reality. The far too prominent politics of rejection in America today necessitates that the rejected must lead a moral revival. We must link up with one another across every dividing line and become a movement to challenge slaveholder religion's distorted moral narrative and revive the heart of American democracy.

THE POLITICS OF REJECTION AND POLICY VIOLENCE AGAINST THE POOR ARE STILL FAR TOO REAL.

We cannot pretend that the politics of rejection are an anomaly caused by just one person. The same God who demanded that we challenge extremism throughout history is calling us to join a revival led by the rejected today. What we read in the ancient text is real in our present context.

Let me see if I can make this live.

In 1967 Dr. Martin Luther King Jr. spoke in this same spirit and theology to issue a warning to America. He preached a sermon that was entitled after a book by

Michael Harrington—*The Other America*. And Dr. King pointed out that there were two Americas. Every city in our country has a kind of dualism—a kind of schizophrenia, he said. And so every city ends up being two cities rather than one. This is Dr. King:

> *There are literally two Americas. One America is beautiful for situation. And, in a sense, this America is overflowing with the milk of prosperity and the honey of opportunity. This America is the habitat of millions of people who have food and material necessities for their*

bodies; and culture and education for their minds; and freedom and human dignity for their spirits. In this America, millions of people experience every day the opportunity of having life, liberty, and the pursuit of happiness in all of their dimensions. And in this America millions of young people grow up in the sunlight of opportunity.

But tragically and unfortunately, there is another America. This other America has a daily ugliness about it that constantly transforms the buoyancy of hope into the fatigue of despair. In this America millions of work-starved men walk the streets daily in search for jobs that do not exist. In this America millions of people find themselves living in rat-infested, vermin-filled slums. In this America people are poor by the millions. They find themselves perishing on a lonely island of poverty in the midst of a vast ocean of material prosperity.

Dr. King was pointing out how the politics of rejection caused so much pain. Fifty years later, the United Nations published its report on extreme poverty in the United States. It painted a damning picture. And it showed that no matter how good the Dow Jones average or the latest job report may seem, we should be wearing sackcloth and ashes to publicly mourn extreme inequality in America.

Philip Alston, the UN Special Rapporteur who acts as the watchdog of extreme poverty around the world, issued a withering critique of the state of America today. Policies that benefit the rich while deregulating companies and neglecting the poor are steering the country toward a dramatic change of direction, blocking poor people from accessing even the most meager necessities. Alston describes a systematic attack on America's welfare programs that is undermining the social safety net for those who can't cope on their own. He went on to say that millions of Americans already struggling to make ends meet face ruination. If food stamps and access to Medicaid are removed and housing subsidies are cut, then the effects on people living on the margin will be drastic. He said that child poverty in America is worse than any other industrialized nation.

Joseph Stiglitz, the Nobel Prize–winning economist, sounded like a prophet when he commented and said, "Can you believe a country where the life expectancy is already in decline particularly among those whose income is low, that that country would be giving tax breaks to billionaires and corporations while leaving millions of Americans without health insurance?" Here we are. And we must be honest that the politics of rejection and policy violence against the poor are still far too real.

Along with the Rev. Dr. Liz Theoharis, I cochair today's Poor People's Campaign: A National Call for Moral Revival, which is bringing together people of every color, creed, sexuality, and immigration status to build a movement led by those who've experienced rejection. Before we launched this campaign in 2018, we conducted an audit of America that revealed 140 million people—43% of this nation—living in poverty and low wealth. According to a report from the Mailman School of Public Health, 250,000 people die from poverty every year in the United States, the richest nation in the history

WE SHOULD BE
WEARING SACKCLOTH
AND ASHES TO
PUBLICLY MOURN
EXTREME INEQUALITY
IN AMERICA TODAY.

of the world. We must be honest that the politics of rejection and policy violence against the poor are still far too real.

I've watched our country cut two trillion dollars for the wealthy, when four hundred people make an average of $97,000 an hour and three people have more money than the bottom 50 percent of Americans combined. And, at the very same time, I've been arrested with people who are fighting for $15 an hour and a union. And I know that the politics of rejection and policy violence against the poor are still far too real.

When 37 million people go without
health care in America—people who pray
not to get sick because they can't afford
treatment—and thousands die every year
because of the lack of access to health
care, forcing preachers, many times, to
preach sermons over bodies that should
not be laying prostrate but should be full
of life; and all the while we know that
the United States is the only one of the
twenty-five wealthiest nations that does
not offer our people health care, we must
be honest that the politics of rejection
and policy violence against the poor are
still far too real.

When indigenous people on reservations face cruel decisions that trace all the way back to wartime treaties; when corporations frack and drill on their sacred lands and poison their aquifers, the politics of rejection and policy violence against the poor are still far too real.

When fifty-three years after Episcopalians and Anglicans and Catholics and Baptists and Methodists marched from churches and were beaten on bridges, black and white, and some died to win voting rights for all God's children, we have open and blatant voter suppression and refusal to restore the Voting Rights Act, the politics of rejection and policy violence against the poor are still far too real.

When a country of immigrants is weaponizing deportation and ripping families apart—even losing the children of migrant families while they brag about doing God's will, I'm telling you, the politics of rejection and policy violence against the poor are still far too real.

When families in Flint, Michigan, like four million other families all over

America, can buy unleaded gas but can't buy unleaded water for their children, the politics of rejection and policy violence against the poor are still far too real.

When a war economy drains social programs and impoverishes communities here at home to destroy and pollute poor communities around the world; when we spend 53 cents of every dollar on war—and only 15 cents on education and health care—the politics of rejection and policy violence against the poor are still far too real.

When the distorted moral narrative

of religious nationalism doesn't follow

the call of Jesus that asks nations,

"When I was hungry, did you feed me?

When I was naked, did you clothe me?

When I was a stranger—when I was an

immigrant, when I was undocumented—

did you care for me?" but instead

preaches a false gospel of division and

building walls and says so much about

what God says so little and so little about

what God says so much, then the politics

of rejection and policy violence against

the poor are still far too real.

When far too many do not see that a Palestinian child is just as important as a Jewish child, and the black child as precious as the white child, then the politics of rejection and policy violence against the poor are still far too real.

Rejection. Poverty. Broken hearts. Bruises. Millions of people who have not been accepted are in our midst. It's not just numbers. I've seen it. We've seen it all over this country. The organizers of today's Poor People's Campaign have seen it. And we live with the nightmares.

I see the Episcopal priest we met with in Aberdeen, Washington, who is trying to minister in a place of only 16,000 human beings, but over 1,000 of them are homeless. The zip code with the largest number of homeless white millennials is in Washington state, despite all of the wealth from Microsoft and Amazon in that part of the country.

In Kentucky, I remember going with white clergy to stand with coal miners who have black lung. The people in Harlan County, one of the thirty poorest counties in America, told us, "Nobody ever comes to see about us."

In Selma, Alabama, I remember Callie Greer, who told us how her daughter died in her arms because Alabama refused to expand health care. I also met Pamela, whose child now has to wear a CPAP machine because of the mold in the trailer that predatory lenders tricked her into buying. Her children have to find places to play in the backyard where sewage isn't coming up.

In my own state of North Carolina, I've seen the rejection. I met little Ezekiel who spoke up for his dad, Pastor Jose, who's been in this country since 1985, but now faces deportation if he steps off the property of a church that offered him sanctuary. There are more sanctuary cases in North Carolina than anywhere else in the country, but all across America, immigrants live in fear because of the politics of rejection.

When I close my eyes, I see Vanessa and her dad, my brother Wensler, of the Apache Nation, who have to fight every day against multinational companies that are destroying their sacred lands for a little bit of copper.

Rosanell Eaton, 95 years old, had to go to court in the twenty-first century to fight for her voting rights after being one of the first black women to register to vote in the South in the 1940s.

Or I see Amy, a poor white woman who is struggling to feed her kids up in the mountains of West Virginia. When the governor of that state expanded teachers' salaries after a wildcat strike, he did a sneaky thing. He expanded the teachers' salaries by cutting Medicaid and cutting food stamps.

I think about Leon, a veteran I met in a homeless camp. He fought for this country. He has a flag planted on a tree branch outside his tent. I asked him why. He said, "Pastor, they allowed me to run billion-dollar pieces of equipment in the military, but now that I've come home, I can't flip a hamburger. I fly the flag so that people will look at the flag and then look underneath the flag and see the rejection that's happening right here in America."

America, we've known rejection in our past. We see rejection around us every day, all over this land. But these ancient texts from the Bible make clear that there is another way.

And it's not some glad morning, when this life is over. It's right now. Did you notice what the Psalmist sang after he announced that the stone that the builders had rejected had now become the chief cornerstone? He said, *"This is the day* that the LORD has made."

Did you hear what Jesus said after he talked about the poor and the broken and those made to feel unsafe? He said, *"You've just heard* Scripture make history."

It has come true in this place. Now is the time for God to act.

And so, we don't have to wait for the stones that have been rejected to become the cornerstones of a new reconstruction movement. I don't know if you've missed it, but the rejected stones are already coming together. By the power of the Spirit, the revival is already afoot.

We've seen it in the Poor People's Campaign. The rejected, they're leading the way. They're coming together and they are declaring that we will reconstruct the economy and the social life of America.

And I'm so glad that God can use the rejected to produce revival. Because I know that there are so many of us who have known rejection. Some have known rejection because of your income, your race, your sexuality. You've known rejection because of who you choose to love. You've known rejection because of how you were born, the color of your skin, the disability you walk with. You've known rejection because somebody

BY THE POWER OF THE SPIRIT, THE REVIVAL IS ALREADY AFOOT.

needed somebody to hate to try to feel good about themselves.

There are people who have known rejection because of faith, because of the lack of faith, because somebody decided in their own ideology that they had a right, a false mandate, to demean your humanity and my humanity given to us only by God.

But I want you to know today, that the stones that the builders rejected are now becoming the cornerstone of this experiment called America. I want you to know today that when the rejected get together in love and in truth and are willing to build a movement with our bodies on the line, we can in fact redeem the soul of the nation from greed, hate, and discrimination.

I want you to know today with no doubt in my mind that I believe by the Holy Ghost when the hands that once picked cotton join Latino hands and progressive white hands, faith hands and labor hands, Asian hands and Native American hands, poor hands and wealthy hands with a conscience, gay hands, straight hands, and trans hands—when all those hands link up together, we can become an instrument of redemption and reconstruction.

So together we have to make sure that hope, not hate, has the last word in the church house and in the state house and even in the White House. Together, we must ensure that all of God's children are respected and treated with dignity. Together, the rejected must redeem and revive the heart of society.

And yes, even the world. Jesus's message of good news to the poor is an announcement for all of us. The rejected must lead. That's why he said, "The Spirit of the Lord is upon me . . ." It's not something we do in our own strength, but by the power of the Spirit. The rejected must lead if we're going to reconstruct America. The rejected have a responsibility to lead.

I believe right now that the soul of America is at stake. The soul of the nation cannot be saved, cannot be sturdy, cannot be properly put together unless the rejected lead the revival and become the chief cornerstones. This has always been true at the heart of our story. Do

WE CAN IN FACT REDEEM THE SOUL OF THE NATION.

you remember that second verse of
"America the Beautiful?"

> *Oh beautiful, for pilgrim feet*
> *Whose stern, impassioned stress*
> *A thoroughfare of freedom beat*
> *Across the wilderness!*
> *America, America!*
> *God mend thine every flaw,*
> *Confirm thy soul in self-control,*
> *Thy liberty in law.*

This will not happen unless the rejected
lead us into a mighty moral revival.
There is no way to mend the flaws of the

nation and be one nation, under God, with liberty and justice for all unless the rejected are at the center. We can't find our way out of the mess we're in with a left focus or a right focus. We've got to refocus on those who have been rejected. Oh, the stones, the stones that the builders rejected have got to become the chief cornerstones. And the preachers must tell it and, with the rejected, show it to the world.

I'm telling you, when the stones that have been rejected come together, something powerful can happen.

Can I preach like I would at home for a minute?

I know the power of getting together because when Moses, who had been rejected, got together with his people and that rod, Pharaoh came down and the Red Sea opened up.

I'm telling you, when Esther and her Uncle Mordecai came together—they had been rejected in the palace—but when Esther said "I'm going to see the king, and if I perish, I perish," they were able to stop the plots of destruction against the people.

When David was overlooked by Samuel and his daddy, he came together with his rock, his slingshot, and his faith. And Goliath fell. They tell me that the headline in *The Jerusalem Post* the next day was "The Bigger They Come, the Harder They Fall."

When three Hebrew children got together way down in the fiery furnace of Babylon, then God cooled the fire down and somebody said they saw a fourth person come stand with them right there in the middle of the flame.

Truth is, whenever the ones who've been rejected have come together down through history and stood together to lead us, justice has never lost. Now, I didn't say justice has never been fought and justice hasn't been beaten up. But justice has never lost.

During slavery, it looked like justice had lost. But when rejected folk like Harriet Tubman and Frederick Douglass and some Quakers and some white Evangelicals got together, they formed a fusion movement and they brought about abolition.

When women were rejected and didn't have the right to vote—Sojourner Truth (rejected), Elizabeth Cady Stanton (rejected), Lucretia Mott (rejected). Each of them was rejected, but when they all got together, they won the right to vote.

Plessy v. Ferguson, the Supreme Court decision that codified Jim Crow segregation, looked like it had won the victory. But when Thurgood Marshall, a rejected lawyer who almost didn't make it out of law school, got together with white lawyers and black lawyers and

Jewish lawyers and Christian lawyers, then an all-white Supreme Court—with one member who had been a part of the KKK—had to vote unanimously that separate but equal was unconstitutional.

It looked like Jim Crow had beaten down justice and it couldn't rise again. But when Rosa Parks (rejected), Martin Luther King Jr. (from a rejected people), Rabbi Heschel (rejected as a Jew), Bayard Rustin (rejected because he was gay), James Reeb (rejected as a race traitor), Viola Liuzzo (rejected because she was a

OH, THERE'S A POWER WHEN THOSE WHO'VE KNOWN REJECTION COME TOGETHER.

white woman willing to stand with black people)—when they all got together, they tore down Jim Crow.

Apartheid in South Africa seemed invincible, but when Nelson Mandela, who was from the rejected, got together with the rejected mothers of South Africa and Bishop Tutu of the Anglican Church and Peter Storey of the Methodists, they turned apartheid around. We like to celebrate those freedom fighters as heroes now, but never forget that God raised them up from among the rejected.

Oh, there's a power when those who've known rejection come together.

I know it biblically. When we come together, we win. I know it historically. When we come together, we win. But let me close by saying that I also know it personally.

Several years ago, some said I would never walk again. They said I'd never get out of a wheelchair. I was thirty years old and had always depended on my legs, but I woke up one morning and couldn't move. I spent three months in a bed at UNC Hospital, not knowing if I would ever get up again. For twelve years I was in a wheelchair or on a walker. But over those dozen years, somehow my mind got together. Then my doctors and my nurses got together. I had a swim coach and some therapists who got together. My church and my family got together.

And when they all got together—when they all got together—God help me, I started to walk again. I started to march again. And I've been marching ever since.

I'm telling you in the name of the God of love, the rejected must lead the movement for love and justice.

The rejected must lead, caring for the poor and living wages and health care and environmental protection. It's the rejected who are going to call us to study war no more. It's the rejected who will demand equal protection under the law. It is the rejected who say that the government must be a government of conscientious aspiration and not authoritarian destruction.

The rejected will lead a movement that says we can do better than protecting guns more than we protect our children. The rejected will lead the revival until

THE REJECTED MUST LEAD THE MOVEMENT FOR LOVE AND JUSTICE.

the killing of black mothers' sons and daughters and the killing of Palestinian mothers' sons and daughters mean as much as the killing of anybody else's children.

The rejected! The rejected! The rejected! They must lead a revival until lives are changed, until systemic racism is dealt with, and classism is dealt with, and homophobia and Islamophobia and xenophobia are dealt with. They must lead the revival until those things move off the stage and make way for love and equality to be the cornerstones of our society, and all human beings are loved with equal regard.

My sisters and brothers, this is the gospel story. It is about what God can do with the rejected. I heard that Jesus came down from heaven, but he was born among the rejected. He came in the form of a servant.

> *He had no beauty or majesty to attract us*
> *   to him,*
> *nothing in his appearance that we should*
> *   desire him.*
> *He was despised and rejected by mankind,*
> *a man of suffering, and familiar with pain.*

Like one from whom people hide their
  faces
he was despised, and we held him in low
  esteem.

Surely he took up our pain
  and bore our suffering,
yet we considered him punished by God,
stricken by him, and afflicted.

But he was pierced for our transgressions,
  he was crushed for our iniquities;
the punishment that brought us peace
  was on him,
and by his wounds we are healed.

Jesus lived among the rejected. He ministered among the rejected. He died and was crucified as rejected, as somebody who was outside the political power structure. But early Sunday morning, from the grave he led a resurrection movement—a revival of love, a revival of justice, a revival of mercy, a revival of grace. And that same power is available to the rejected today. Revival power! Resurrection power! Love power! Mercy power! Telling the truth power!

That's why every day I'm praying by the Spirit, "Lord, send it on down. Lord, let

the Holy Ghost come on down! Use us,
Lord. Use the rejected, Lord. Use us,
Lord! By the Spirit, bring us together."

And when we all get together; when all of
us who love to love get together;

when all of us who love justice get
together;

when all of us who love lifting people up
get together;

when all of us who love mercy get
together;

when we all get together, what a day!

What a day! What a day!

What a day! What a day!

What a day of revival it will be!

THE POOR PEOPLE'S CAMPAIGN

A NATIONAL CALL FOR A MORAL REVIVAL

In 1968, Rev. Dr. Martin Luther King, Jr. and thousands of Americans, alarmed at their government's blindness to human need, launched the Poor People's Campaign. As they marched up from the nation's neglected shadows, Dr. King paused to answer a plea for support from sanitation workers on strike in Memphis. There an assassin snatched his life on April 4.

Brokenhearted, this "freedom church of the poor" gathered by the thousands in Washington. They erected "Resurrection City," their encampment on the National Mall, to demand that their government address bitter poverty in the wealthiest nation in the world. They confronted fundamental questions about America's moral and Constitutional vision for all its people, regardless of their wealth, race, gender or national origin. They demanded attention to the hungry children and inadequate schools from Appalachia to the Mississippi Delta to the devastated inner cities across America. They bore moral witness against America's long, pointless, and immoral war in Vietnam, and tried hard to be heard as they carried their testimony forward into public life. The hard history that compelled them to "pray with their feet," as Rabbi Abraham Heschel said, also compelled many Americans to ask whether the republic for which they stood would ever stand for them.

Over fifty years later, beset by deepening poverty, ecological devastation, systemic racism, and an economy harnessed to seemingly endless war, "the Poor People's Campaign: A National Call for Moral Revival" likewise beckons our nation to higher ground. We call upon our society to see the predicaments of the most vulnerable among us and to halt the destruction of America's moral vision. Hundreds of thousands across the nation today stand on the shoulders of that "freedom church" of 1968. We turn to America's history—and to the realities of our own time—not to wallow in a fruitless nostalgia of pain. We seek instead to redeem a democratic promise enshrined in the U.S. Constitution and the Declaration of Independence, yet even more deeply rooted in the living ingredients of our own lives and embodied in the countless and largely unacknowledged grassroots activists who have labored to lift those founding documents to their full meaning. We come to remind our nation what truths we hold to be self-evident. We come to remind our nation what values we hold dear. In Washington and at state capitols around the country, we hope to make a new moral witness from our love for what Maya Angelou called "these-yet-to-be united states."

Dr. King and a multicolored quilt of God's children invoked America's better angels, confident that the keys to our predicaments lay in the hearts of our people. None of our diverse faith traditions celebrate denying food to hungry children or devoting trillions to war and pennies to want. No moral vision embraces the denial of health care to our fellow human beings. Many Americans appear to have forgotten their own values and become blind to the needs of other human beings, even those they may still hold in their hearts.

These deep forms of myopia reflect still deeper failures of memory. "The struggle of man against entrenched power," writes novelist Milan Kundera, "is the struggle of memory against forgetting." Few recall that the war in Vietnam drained away many of the resources for the War on Poverty, which did much but could have done much more. "The bombs in Vietnam explode at home," Dr. King said. Fewer still recall the prophetic voice of the Poor People's Campaign and that Dr. King died organizing a nonviolent revolution to push America toward a social ethos grounded in love. "We are called upon to raise certain basic questions about the whole society," King preached before his assassination. "We must recognize that we can't solve our problem now until there is a radical redistribution of economic and political power." It is time that we turn to our past in order to understand our present, and then turn forward together to build a better future.

As shining and crucial the roles of Dr. King and other notable leaders have been, neither the Poor People's Campaign of 1968 nor our cause of love, mercy, and justice today rolled forward on the gifts of a great leader. Our victories in the timeless cause of love and democracy have always required the devotion of thousands of ordinary people, local communities, grassroots groups, prophetic churches, and organizing traditions. In that spirit, the new Poor People's Campaign brings together people from all walks of life to demand that our country see the poor in our streets, confront the damage to our natural environment, and ponder the ailments of a nation that year after year spends more money on endless war than on human need. The time has come to stand together and make a national call for moral revival.

To learn more about the Poor People's Campaign and join us, register for the movement at poorpeoplescampaign.org or by texting "MORAL" to 90975.

FUNDAMENTAL PRINCIPLES OF THE POOR PEOPLE'S CAMPAIGN

1. We are rooted in a moral analysis based on our deepest religious and constitutional values that demand justice for all. Moral revival is necessary to save the heart and soul of our democracy.

2. We are committed to lifting up and deepening the leadership of those most affected by systemic racism, poverty, the war economy, and ecological devastation and to building unity across lines of division.

3. We believe in the dismantling of unjust criminalization systems that exploit poor communities and communities of color and the transformation of the "War Economy" into a "Peace Economy" that values all humanity.

4. We believe that equal protection under the law is non-negotiable.

5. We believe that people should not live in or die from poverty in the richest nation ever to exist. Blaming the poor and claiming that the United States does not have an abundance of resources to overcome poverty are false narratives used to perpetuate economic exploitation, exclusion, and deep inequality.

6. We recognize the centrality of systemic racism in maintaining economic oppression must be named, detailed, and exposed empirically, morally, and spiritually. Poverty and economic inequality cannot be understood apart from a society built on white supremacy.

7. We aim to shift the distorted moral narrative often promoted by religious extremists in the nation from issues like prayer in school, abortion, and gun rights to one that is concerned with how our society treats the poor, those on the margins, women, LGBTQIA folks, workers, immigrants, the disabled, and the sick; with equality and representation under the law; and with the desire for peace, love, and harmony within and among nations.

8. We will build up the power of people and state-based movements to serve as a vehicle for a powerful moral movement in the country and to transform the political, economic, and moral structures of our society.

9. We recognize the need to organize at the state and local level—many of the most regressive policies are being passed at the state level, and these policies will have long and lasting effect, past even executive orders. The movement is not from above but below.

10. We will do our work in a nonpartisan way—no elected officials or candidates get the stage or serve on the State Organizing Committee of the Campaign. This is not about left and right, Democrat or Republican, but about right and wrong.

11. We uphold the need to do a season of sustained moral direct action as a way to break through the tweets and shift the moral narrative. We are demonstrating the power of people coming together across issues and geography and putting our bodies on the line to the issues that are affecting us all.

12. The Campaign and all its participants and endorsers embrace nonviolence. Violent tactics or actions will not be tolerated.

Rev. Dr. William J. Barber II

is the President & Senior Lecturer of
Repairers of the Breach and Cochair of the
Poor People's Campaign: A National Call
for Moral Revival. He is also Bishop with
the College of Affirming Bishops and Faith
Leaders and Senior Pastor of Greenleaf
Christian Church, Disciples of Christ in
Goldsboro, North Carolina.

Rev. Dr. Barber served as president of the
North Carolina NAACP, the largest state
conference in the South, from 2006–2017
and currently sits on the National NAACP
Board of Directors. A former Mel King Fellow
at MIT, he is currently Visiting Professor
of Public Theology and Activism at Union

Theological Seminary and is a Senior Fellow at Auburn Seminary. Rev. Dr. Barber is regularly featured in media outlets such as MSNBC, CNN, *The New York Times*, *The Washington Post*, *The Guardian* and *The Nation*. He is the recipient of the Puffin Award, the Franklin D. Roosevelt Four Freedoms Award, and was a 2018 MacArthur Fellow.